Still DESTINED FOR GREATNESS

BISHOP A.G. MULLEN, JR.

Published By:
Jasher Press & Co.
www.jasherpress.com
P.O. Box 14520
New Bern, NC 28561

Copyright© 2011
Interior Text Design by Pamela S. Almore
Cover Design by Pamela S. Almore

ISBN: 978-0615535593
Still Destined For Greatness

Second Edition
Printed and bound in the United States of America
Copyright © 2011 A.G. Mullen, Jr.

Still DESTINED FOR GREATNESS

BISHOP
A.G. MULLEN, JR.

WWW.ALBC.ORG

JASHER PRESS & CO.

TABLE OF CONTENTS

ACKNOWLEDGEMENTS

Very few people will ever understand the awesome task of pasturing a flock of God's people. It is probably one of the most rewarding assignments that one can have in life, but also one of the most burdensome responsibilities that an individual can obtain. One thing is for sure, I know that God has called me into the Gospel ministry. For almost 33 years, I have been preaching the Gospel of our Lord and Savior Jesus Christ. I have been pasturing for approximately 29 years and this particular church, Abundant Life International Baptist Cathedral that I am now pasturing, was founded by me 16 years ago.

God has blessed me to venture overseas into southern Africa and God has granted me the privilege to plant and nurture congregations in Zimbabwe and South Africa. During these years, many lives have been touched and deliverance has taken place in far remote areas of Africa.

Spiritual sons and daughters have been licensed and ordained to preach the Word of God and pastor his people under my spiritual oversight. God has even elevated me to the office of bishop with the responsibility of pasturing pastors throughout the entire state, but none of these assignments has challenged me quite like the challenge of writing my first book.

All these years, I have spent most of my time doing the work of ministry without recognizing the importance of putting it in writing, but God has now released me to write about what I have experienced and accomplished by his grace.

Therefore, I would like to acknowledge my dear wife C-Pastor Vanessa H. Mullen as the number one motivating factor in me completing this first book. Thanks to my children, who I love very dearly, Canita, Krystal and Gerard. Thanks to my mother and father, Aubrey and Bernice Mullen for bringing me into this world and raising me up. Also, I would like to thank my Virtual Executive Assistant Gwendolyn Jackson for helping me to create a legible manuscript. Thanks to Jasher Press for being diligent and persistent in making this revised edition a reality.

Last but not least, I would like to dedicate this book to my deceased son Christopher Lamont Mullen and my beautiful grandchildren; Na'Jaria, Abria, Kristeon, Nyjah, Christopher and Aydan.

FOREWORD

Our attitudes set the stage for what will occur in our live-good attitude, good results, fair attitude, fair results, poor attitude, and poor results. Each of us shapes his or her own life; and the shape of our lives will be and are determined by our attitude.

The majority of people go through life with their mental attitudes dominated by fears, anxieties, and worries, seeing only the appearance of failure, which somehow has a way of becoming a reality. Millions of people continually crashed on the rocks of bad consequences, often suffering irreparable damage, because they allow themselves to get caught in rough waters without staying focused. A right mental attitude is the fixed compass assuring that every experience, whether it is pleasant or unpleasant, yields some form of benefit. Only a right mental attitude pays off in the affairs of our everyday living. I have watched over the years as this recognized Father and Pastor (now Author), has grown though his personal experiences with life and God. I admire the fact that Bishop Mullen so freely and carelessly shares the revelation of his experiences through this publication that is sure to bless many lives for a long time.

If you will change your thinking, you will change your life. The power of thought, depending on how it is used, is the most dangerous and the most beneficial force available to man. Through this power, man has built great empires of civilization. Through the same power, other men have trampled down these empires like so many insignificant pieces of clay. By its application, man rises to seize his opportunity. And through neglect or misuse of this same power, man has turned his back on opportunities, becoming a puppet of his environment, a slave to his circumstances. With all of the negative bad news that fills our hearts and minds it's refreshing to hear the confirming words of Almighty God though one of His servants who dares to Divinely Declare that I've been destined for Greatness!

Every creation of man, whether it is good or bad, is created first in a pattern of thought. All ideas, plans and purposes are created in thought. As men search all their lives for worldly riches, they fail to realize that "the source" of all they would ever desire is already within their reach and under their control, awaiting only their recognition and use. Bishop Mullen is used of God to highlight aspects of the lives of biblical characters who experienced some of the same things you and I are experiencing today.

The power of persistence is characteristic of all men and women who have achieved greatness. It is not so much brilliance of intellect, talent, or resources as it is persistency of effort and constancy of purpose that draws greatness to the individual. Those who succeed in life are the men and women who keep their shoulders to the wheel, who do not believe themselves overly talented, but who realize that if they are ever to accomplish anything of value, they must do so by determined and persistent effort.

Persistence means conviction, enthusiasm, perseverance, and courage in the face of obstructions. Above all, it means never stopping, never giving up, and never giving in! You are destined for Greatness.

Constantly Amazed,

Bishop Darryl S. Brister
Beacon Light International Ministries
Apostle/Overseer

INTRODUCTION

This book is about becoming all that God has destined for us to become as believers in Christ. The scriptures reveal certain biblical principles unto us that will guide us to great success, if we will follow them. Certainly, I do not attempt to exhaust the studies of success as it relates to the Bible in this rendering, but each chapter will provide some interesting information concerning biblical success. One very powerful lesson illustrated in this book, is that one does not have to start out great to end up great and that we should not despise small beginnings. This principle is relevant to my life, as I look at how far God has brought me from. He has told me on more than one occasion to "just do it;" sometimes feeling inadequate, sometimes trembling in fear and apprehension, but still I would only hear Him say, "Just Do It." So I would always start out small, but because I was willing to start out with minimal resources, He would always do something miraculous and great.

Someone once said that perception was everything. This may not be totally true but it has much credence. For instance, in this book I discuss the importance of looking at life from God's point of view. God sees something about us that sometimes is totally different from what we see about ourselves. God always has a way of seeing the best in us regardless of our circumstances or situations. And, it is certainly His desire to bring the best out of us.

Inside each and every one of us, there is a gift or gifts that God has endowed us with. It is the thing that causes us to get up in the morning and look at life from a very positive point of view. It is the very thing that motivates us to live and to thrive in the mist of adversity. In this book, I will talk about the importance of being a problem solver and not a problem maker. God stresses the importance of using one's gift, for it will make room for one and bring one before great people.

These and many other topics you will find in this book will become instrumental tools to help you to understand you are destined for greatness. Now keep reading and you will see that you are positioned for greatness and prosperity in chapter one.

CHAPTER ONE

POSITIONED FOR GREATNESS AND PROSPERITY

Then Pharaoh sent and called Joseph, and they brought
Him hastily out of the dungeon: and he shaved
Himself; and changed his raiment, and came in unto Pharaoh.
And Pharaoh said unto Joseph, I have dreamed a dream, and
there is none that can interpret it: and I have say of thee that
though canst understand a dream to interpret it. And Joseph
answered Pharaoh, saying, It is not me: God shall give Pharaoh
an answer of peace.
Genesis 41:14-16

Joseph was the first child of his mother, Rachel and certainly, he was his father's favorite son. This was made very clear from the coat of many colors that his father earnestly lavished upon him. However, this unusual favor coming from his father created serious problems for the whole family as time went on. Joseph's ten older brothers hated him with a passion because he was Jacob's favorite boy and because he had dreams, that {when interpreted}, placed him in dominion over his other brothers.

Eventually things just came to a grand finale and Joseph's brothers could not take it any longer. Jacob, the Father had sent Joseph to check on his brothers who were tending the flocks in the field.

When Joseph found his brothers, they seized him, attempted to murder him. His brothers would have murdered him if it had not been for Reuben who opposed it. Instead, they cast him into a pit and finally sold him into slavery.

He was sold into Potiphar an Egyptian officer. And while serving Potiphar he was given the most powerful position in the household. However, while on his way to being positioned for greatness the enemy tried to get him to abort his destiny.

This potential abortion of Joseph's destiny occurs in Genesis 39:7-20. The scripture tells us that the master's wife could not keep her eyes off of Joseph and she insisted that Joseph would have sexual relations with her. Actually, she represented the temptation or trail that has been designed to make us abort our promises. Whenever we are on our way to greatness, the devil has someone or something to detour us if we allow it.

But Joseph refused according to verse 8, he told her, "Look, my master trusts me with everything in his entire household."

All it would have taken was one wrong move and Joseph's destiny could have been aborted, but Joseph said, "I can't do this great wickedness, and sin against God."

Brothers and sisters, God has predestined your future, but you must be extremely careful that you pray and watch for potential traps that Satan has planted all around you to distract you and detour you from greatness. In verse [10] it says, "And it come to pass, as she spake to Joseph day by day, that he hearkened not unto her, to lie by her, or to be with her. [11] And it came to pass about this time that Joseph went into the house to do his business; and there was none of the men of the house there within. (This was the first mistake that Joseph made, because he had no one to cover for him.)

[12] And she caught him by his garment, saying, lie with me; and he left his garment in her hand, and fled, and got him out.

[13] And it came to pass, when she saw that he had left his garment in her hand, and was fled forth, [14] That she called unto the men of her house, and spake unto them, saying, see, he hath brought in an Hebrew unto us to mock us; he came in unto me to lie with me, and I cried with a loud voice: [15] And it came to pass, when he heard that I lifted up my voice and cried, that he left his garment with me, and fled, and got him out.

You see, Joseph had spurned her, and her pride was hurt so she lied on him . . .

And you know the rest of the story how the Master, Potiphar believed her lies and Joseph was thrown into prison. It doesn't matter how good we live at times, there is always going to be some people who want to believe a lie about us and they will attempt to abort our destiny. But Joseph somehow realized his destiny wasn't in man's hand, but God's.

Notice: Gen. 39:9, "There is none greater in this house than I; neither hath he kept back anything from me but thee, because thou art his wife: how then can I do this great wickedness, and sin against God?"

You must realize that your destiny is in God's hands and not man's (because Joseph didn't sin against God, Satan couldn't stop his destiny).

But it was in prison that Joseph truly positioned himself for greatness. Joseph used his gift of dream interpretation to prosper himself. And according to the text, the chief butler finally remembered Joseph's ability as the King; Pharaoh had a dream about the future . . .

To understand the main thought of this lesson we must see the background of this chapter . . . Genesis 40:1-23

The background of this chapter starts out with the butler and baker offending the king. And Pharaoh was extremely angry with both the chief butler and chief baker. He threw them both in prison alongside Joseph. And Joseph had the oversight of them. Both men had dreams and neither man could figure his dream out, but Joseph knew that God could give him the interpretation of it.

Verses 9-23: [9] And the chief butler told his dream to Joseph, and said to him, In my dream, behold, a vine was before me; [10] and in the vines were three branches: and it was as though it budded, and her blossoms shot forth; and the clusters thereof brought forth ripe grapes: [11] and Pharaoh's cup was in my hand: and I took the grapes, and pressed them into Pharaoh's cup, and I gave the cup into Pharaoh's hand. [12] and Joseph said unto him, This is the interpretation of it: The three branches are three days: [13] Yet within three days, shall Pharaoh lift up thine head, and restore thee unto thy place: and thou shalt deliver Pharaoh's cup into his hand, after the former manner when thou was his butler. *[14] But think on me when it shall be well with thee, and shew kindness, I pray thee, unto me, and make mention of me unto Pharaoh, and bring me out of this house: [15] for indeed I was stolen away out of the land of the Hebrews: and here also have I done nothing that they should put me into the dungeon.*

Here Joseph really meant for the butler not to forget about him.

And of course, we know that the bakers dream was interpreted by Joseph and the baker met his demise.

But verse 23 tells us what the butler initially did: *[23] Yet did not the chief butler remember Joseph, but forgot him.* It's a shame, but the people we do the most for are the quickest to forget us.

But it was only after the King had a disturbing dream that the butler remembered about Joseph . . . Genesis 41:11-12.

The butler put it like this "And we dreamed a dream in one night, I and he; (the baker) we dreamed each man according to the interpretation of his dream. [12] And there was there with us a young man, a Hebrew, servant to the captain of the guard; and we told him, and he interpreted to us our dreams; to each man according to his dream he did interpret. So the butler remembered Joseph ... and this gave the king some hope.

Genesis 41:14-32: When you remain faithful in proper alignment, the King is going to want to see you. You won't have to go looking for a blessing the blessing will find you. When people know you have favor with the King they will move swiftly on your behalf. People who had dogged you before will now lift you up. The text says that Joseph shaved himself and hanged his raiment and came in unto Pharaoh. He literally dressed for success. You have to carry yourself like you are somebody, because you are somebody. And Pharaoh said unto Joseph, I have dreamed a dream, and there is none that can interpret it.

There's always going to be a problem that others can't solve. The mechanic knows that most people can't tune up their cars anymore. The auto body repairman knows that most patients don't know what medicine to prescribe. **When you are prepared and in the right position favor comes into your life.**

Prosperity is when your Gift or Talent meets Opportunity. Pharaoh said, *"and I have heard say of thee, that thou canst understand a dream to interpret it. When you're in position, someone who can bless you would have heard about you and your ability.* You should position yourself so that someone hears about you. And Joseph answered Pharaoh, saying, it is not in me: God shall give Pharaoh an answer of peace. Remember who gives you the power or wisdom.

You See! Joseph gave the glory to God. Pharaoh goes on and begins to disclose his dream unto Joseph. He says he stood on the bank of the river and he says I saw seven cows that were fat and well fed. And then I saw seven other cows skinny and malnourished. And the malnourished cows ate up the fat and well fed cows. And even after the malnourished cows ate the fat ones, they were still malnourished. And then Pharaoh said that seven bad ears of corn ate up seven good ears and none of his magicians could figure it out. There is always going to be a problem or challenge that only God can solve through you. Ask

God to allow you to solve them. And so Joseph's gift made room for him as he interpreted Pharaoh's dream. He explains that the two dreams have the same meaning just illustrated in different ways. He says there's going to be seven years of plenty throughout the land but afterwards there will be seven years of famine.

This gave Joseph great favor with the king, because he was able to solve this problem. He had so much favor, that the King placed him over the national product of the land of Egypt.

Has anybody heard about you? Have you solved a problem and someone heard about you? What problem could you solve today? Whose life could be blessed from your gift today? Have you positioned yourself for greatness? Have you positioned yourself for someone to hear about you? Are you maximizing the moment? Are you purposed driven? Have you positioned yourself for greatness? To position yourself for greatness you must allow the Lord to use you. To position yourself for greatness you must not despise small beginnings. To position yourself for greatness you must be faithful unto a few things. To position yourself for greatness you must know where you want to go. To position yourself for greatness, don't make that one wrong move that will distract you from your destiny!

CHAPTER TWO

THE SPIRITUAL LAW OF GUARANTEED SUCCESS

Then Jesus told his disciples a parable to show
them that they should always pray and not give up.
He said: "In a certain town there was a judge who neither feared
God nor cared about men. And there was a widow in that town
who kept coming to him with the plea, 'Grant me justice against
my adversary.'
"For some time he refused. But finally he said to himself,
'Even though I don't fear God or care about men, yet because
this widow keeps bothering me, I will see that she gets justice, so
that she won't eventually wear me out with her coming!'" And
the Lord said, "Listen to what the unjust judge says. And will not
God bring about justice for his chosen ones, who cry out to him
day and night? Will he keep putting them off? I tell you, he will
see that they get justice, and quickly.
However, when the Son of Man comes, will he find faith
on the earth?"
Luke 18:1-8 (NIV)

Here in this chapter, we see there comes a time that you must push your way through to come out successfully.
Two things the Law of Guaranteed Success says according to Matthew 7:7-11, Luke 8:1-8:

The law of guaranteed success says that I must have desire. If you want something out of life then you must be ambitious enough to go after it. You must have a desire.

(vs. 7) Therefore, if desire is necessary for me to be successful, the devil will work on killing my desire. You must be willing to ask for what you want and if it doesn't come easily don't give in and don't give up. Begin to look for the answer or solution. And if after looking, you still don't find it, you must be willing to knock until the door is open.

God has something in store for us but He only <u>responds to our faith and not our wishes (vs. 8).</u> You can wish all day long for God to deliver you, but it won't happen. You must step out in faith and believe that God is able to do what He said He could do. You need to be aware that God is not holding you back but He <u>really wants to see you blessed (vs.).</u>

The law of guaranteed success says that I must be persistent.

Now it is a known fact that prayer changes things. God tells us in His word that we <u>should always pray </u>(vs. 1). We should pray without ceasing but we should also travail in prayer. Like a woman having a baby we must push some things out in the spirit realm. There are some promises being aborted because we are not travailing but instead we are wailing. God wants our prayers to be proactive and not reactive. He wants us to <u>never give up </u>(vs. 1). Quitting is not an option for us as believers. If something is His will and it's in the word, we should not quit or give up on Him. People now days give up to easily. That's one of our greatest problems. <u>We must be persistent</u> if we expect to be over comers (vs. 2-5). And you must know that God will always <u>answer prayer</u> and not only will He answer it but He will <u>answer it speedily</u> (vs. 6-8).

Now there are two other laws closely related to The Law of GUARANTEED SUCCESS, the Law of Reciprocity and the Law of Use. These are also very important principles of the kingdom. The Law of Reciprocity says that you can make sure that good things come into your life by practicing the golden rule. Essentially this law says that whatever you give will come back to you again; therefore you need to sow the right kinds of seeds if you want a good return. And the law of use, that says you must use what you have to get what you want. You can only prosper if you utilize what you have. This scripture illustrates my point. (Matthew 25:14-30), For the kingdom of heaven is as a man traveling into a far country, who called his own servants, and delivered unto them his goods. [15] And unto one, he gave five talents, to another two, and to another one; to every man according to his several ability; and straightway took his journey. [16] Then he that had received the five talents went and traded with the same, and made them other five talents. [17] And likewise he that had receive two, he also gained other two. [18] But he that had received one went and digged in the earth, and hid his lord's money. [19] After a long time the lord of those servants cometh, and reckoneth . . . [29] For unto everyone that hath shall be given, and he shall have abundance: but from him that hath not shall be taken away even that which he hath.

Our text shows us we don't have to give up. The scripture declares that Jesus spoke a parable unto them. This was the Master's favorite method of teaching. A parable was an earthly story with a divine or heavenly meaning. I'm sure you remember the parable of the prodigal son. This story talks about the young man who is so eager to leave home and experience the world. He gets his portion of the inheritance and squanders it on riotous living. He finds out that after all his money is gone so is all his so called friends.

Later, somewhere along the line, he comes to his senses

and realizes that he doesn't have to live the way that he's living. He repents and heads home, but without him realizing it, his father is waiting for him. This story clearly illustrates how God is waiting on us to repent and return back home. There are many other parables such as the lost sheep and the lost coin, but Jesus uses these stories to teach divine principles.

Now this parable had a special teaching that it tried to illustrate. Its main purpose was to teach men that they should always pray and not faint. We should always pray and not give up. No matter how hard the test or how difficult the problem, we must always believe that God can make a way somehow.

Saints today, just as saints of old must always pray and never give up. I know that sometimes our test and trials seem almost unbearable, but we must never give up. The Lord will make a way somehow. The Word of God declares that God will not allow more to be put on us than we can bear. Every trial and every test the Lord already foreknew that you could handle it, because He gave Satan boundaries and limitations and told him that he could only go so far. Saints we must always pray because He may not come when we want Him to come but He's always on time. He's never been late with the groceries, He's never been late on the rent; He's never been late for a doctor's appointment. He's always right on time!

Our first character in our text is a judge. He had the awesome responsibility of interpreting the law. He should have a devout Jew who reverences God, but the scripture gives two very important descriptions about this man. Number one, He did not fear God or he had no reverence for God and, number two he had no regards for his fellow man. It's questionable about this man's employment. How could he actually be interpreting a law from a God that he had no reverence for. It kind of reminds me of toady. We have people sitting in the Supreme Court determining the destiny of our lives but they have no God in them. They don't reverence God and they could care less about you and me.

I hate to say it but it's true, many of our citizens today are just like this unjust judge. They do not reverence God and they have no regard for their fellow man. Our society is filled full of atheists and agnostics, unbelievers and doubters. Many men think that there are no absolutes in this world and that they can do their own thing. Our society is filled with anarchy everywhere. Lawlessness fills the land. People are sacrilegious and disregard everything that is sacred.

The TV shows and talk shows are full of jokes and cracks about God. Nothing is sacred anymore. People use the Lord's name in vain and think absolutely nothing of it. Gays and lesbians are taking over and cults are on the rampage. Abortions and murders are at an all time high. And our lands are filled with terror as terrorists threaten our way of life all over the world. We need to reverence God and regard our fellow man.

Our second character and most important character in our text is this widow woman. When we think about the New Testament society, the widow woman was the most abused and dejected woman of that day. The abuse and dejection of the widows had come to an apex in the sixth chapter of the book of Acts to the extent that we see deacons coming on the scene to primarily serve the widows. Paul admonishes the New Testament saints to take care of the widows of the church who were sixty years of age and older.

The scripture says that she had to go before this unjust

character who called himself a judge. Too often, Christians have to go before the unjust. Too often good people have to submit to wicked people who are in power. That's why we need to come off our islands of isolation and be the salt of the earth and the lights of the world that God has called us to be. We should be actively involved in every area of life. There should be Christians involved in politics, Christians in business, Christians in medical research, Christian lawyers and businessmen. Christians should be involved in education and all major systems of our society. The righteous need representation as well.

The bible says that this woman wanted justice or recompense. She says avenge me of my adversary. Who would be an adversary of an old widow woman? There were sick individuals back then and there are still many sick individuals today. Maybe this woman was cheated by some slick businessman. Slick businessmen are cheating widows and women even today. Slick car repairmen are cheating widows today. Con artists are soliciting funds from the elderly. Insurance agents are charging the elderly outrageous premiums and new scams are being thought of on a daily basis by dishonest people all over the world.

The bible says that some time had expired and the unjust judge gave things more thought. God will cause the unrighteous to give things another thought. The wicked will end up blessing you and won't even know why. The bible says, "When a man's ways please the Lord, even his enemies will be at peace with him."

This widow troubled the judge. She operated in the principle called the Law of Guaranteed Success. She visited this man's courtroom every day until she got results. She kept on and on appealing her case because she knew she was in the right. She insisted that what was hers was hers and no devil in hell was going to steal her joy. She had a made up mind.

My brothers and sisters you must operate in the Law of Guaranteed Success also. You must visit God's courtroom day after day until you get results. The bible tells us to come boldly before the throne of grace and let our request be known unto God. You must insist that what's yours is yours and you shall not be denied. You must know that our God is about avenging us of our adversary, the devil. And as far as I can see in the end, we win.

[6] And the Lord said, Hear what the unjust judge saith. [7] And shall not God avenge his own elect, which cry day and night unto him, though he bear long with them? [8] I tell you that He will avenge them speedily. Nevertheless, when the Son of man cometh, shall he find faith on the earth? [KJV]

If God can find faith, He'll answer your prayer. If God can find faith, He'll have regards for you. If God can find faith; He'll avenge you of the adversary. If God can find faith, He'll cause people to change their minds. If God can find faith, He'll answer your prayers speedily!

The purpose of this chapter was to reveal to the believer that there is a spiritual law that will ensure that the results that we desire will and shall come to pass. It is the Law of GUARANTEED SUCCESS or the Law of Never Giving Up. From this spiritual principle, we see that God wants us to determine our own destinies by operating within His principles rather than giving in or giving up without a spiritual fight. The Bible tells us that the kingdom of God suffers violence and the violent take it by force. If we are going to have victory in this life then we must not give in too easily. We must never give in or give up on God.

The devil thought that he was in control and that he had us

27

right in the palms of his hands. He literally thought that if he could bring enough tragedy into our lives that we would eventually give up on our faith and cease to put our trust in God. He knew that he had but a short time so he intensified his evil works in our lives. But brothers and sisters never give in and never give up on God, the Word promises us that God will always come through.

Man should never give up on God, but pray always and pray through until his change comes.

Never give up on God because prayer changes things. Never give up on God because the Law of Guaranteed Success still operates today. Never give up on God because He will change people's minds. Success is guaranteed when we refuse to give in or give up. Success is guaranteed when we keep on praying through.

Satan's main objective now is to cause us to give up but throughout history, some have refused to accept his program for their lives. Out of the state of Illinois came an individual who refused to give in and faint. It is said that he made a run for the Illinois legislature in 1832 and lost. He made a run for the U.S. Senate and lost. He made a bid for the presidency to no avail. He ran again in 1834, 1836, 1838, and 1840, and he won all four times. Also, in 1846 he ran for the United States House of Representatives and won. An in 1856, he received support for the Republican Vice-Presidential nomination. On November 6, 1860, he became the 16th President of the United States. He stood for the union and he stood against slavery. His name is Abraham Lincoln. He persevered; in spite of the odds against him, and came out victorious. Whatever is getting the most of you, will you believe in the power of prayer and trust in an immutable spiritual law from God, called the Law of Guaranteed Success!

CHAPTER THREE

DON'T LET YOUR DISOBEDIENCE REMOVE YOU FROM YOUR DESTINY

On the seventh day, when King Xerxes was in high spirits from wine, he commanded the seven eunuchs who served him— Mehuman, Biztha, Harbona, Bigtha, Abagtha, Zethar and Carcas- to bring before him Queen Vashti, wearing her royal crown, in order to display her beauty to the people and nobles, for she was lovely to look at. But when the attendants delivered the king's command, Queen Vashti refused to come. Then the king became furious and burned with anger. Since it was customary for the king to consult experts in matters of law and justice, he spoke with the wise men who understood the times and were closest to the king—Carshena, Shethar, Admatha, Tarshish, Meres, Marsena and Memucan, the seven nobles of Persia and Media who had special access to the king and were highest in the kingdom. "According to law, what must be done to Queen Vashti?" he asked. "She has not obeyed the command of King Xerxes that the eunuchs have taken to her." Then Memucan replied in the presence of the king and the nobles, "Queen Vashti has done wrong, not only against the king but also against all the nobles and the peoples of all the provinces of King Xerxes. For the queen's conduct will become known to all the women, and so they will despise their husbands and say, 'King Xerxes commanded Queen Vashti to be brought before him, but she would not come.' This very day the Persian and Median women of the nobility who have heard about the queen's conduct

*will respond to all the king's nobles in the same way. There will
be no end of disrespect and discord. "Therefore, if it pleases the
king, let him issue a royal decree and let it be written in the laws
of Persia and Media, which cannot be repealed, that Vashti is
never again to enter the presence of King Xerxes. Also let the
king give her royal position to someone else who is better than
she.*
Ester 1:10-19(NIV)

Through the study of the word of God and through experience, I have found out the quickest and surest way to abort destiny is to get into a state of disobedience. The enemy works overtime in trying to get us to exalt ourselves and think more highly of ourselves than we ought to. On the contrary, God's desire is that we would reach our full potential and fulfill our destinies with few interruptions and minimum distractions. It is so important we hear the Lord and obey the Lord without reservations. To have reservations is to display contempt and God does not take contempt too kindly. More than ever before, we should be trying to find favor with the king rather than constantly testing his ability to offer us grace and mercy. If we continue to test God all the time, eventually this grace and mercy is going to run out and we will forfeit our privileges with God. In this chapter, we can see how obedience elevates one and how disobedience demotes another.

This story begins during the reign of King Xerxes, who ruled over 127 provinces stretching from India to Ethiopia. He was a very powerful and influential king. His empire was situated in the fortress of Susa and in the third year of his reign, he threw this tremendous party for all his princes, officials, military officers and noblemen that lasted for six months. It was just an opulent display of great wealth and glory. After that party was over, the king threw another party for his palace servants and officials that lasted seven days in the courtyard of the palace garden. He was just a jolly good fellow, as it seemed. Everything was decorated with the most exquisite taste. There were linen hangings of white and blue with purple ribbons and silver rings embedded in marble pillars. There were gold and silver couches standing on mosaic pavement of porphyry, marble, mother of pearl and other costly stones. Even the drinks were poured into gold goblets of every sort and there was an abundance of wine just as the king had ordered. The only restriction was that no one should be made to drink more than he wanted but if they wanted more, they could drink as much as they wanted.

While this party was going on, the Queen Vashti was throwing her party for the women at the same time. Now it was about the seventh day of the feast when the king summoned his wife. He wanted to show her off to all the men. He wanted them to gaze on her beauty and dream of her, for she was a very beautiful woman. But when they gave Queen Vashti the order from the King, she refused to budge. She remained where she was and did not come unto him. Of course, this infuriated the King and he burned with anger. What could have been going through Vashti's mind? Didn't she know what she was doing? Was she a glutton for punishment? Or did she forget where the king had brought her from.

Like many of us, we so easily forget what the Lord has done for us and when He calls us we refuse or will not answer. Was there an element of pride that had swollen up into Vashti? For the Word tells us that pride goeth before the fall and God cannot stand the haughty spirit. The king was really thrown back with this act of disobedience. He was totally shocked and so he needed advice. So he called for his seven top advisors and associates in the kingdom and asked them for advice.

And so this chapter also shows us that disobedience can cause you to abort the future that God has in store for you.

Read the NLT (verses 16-19)

[16] Memucan answered the king and his princes, "Queen Vashti has wronged not only the king but also every official and citizen throughout your empire. [17] Women everywhere will begin to despise their husbands when they learn that Queen Vashti has refused to appear before the king. [18] Before this day is out, the wife of every one of us, your officials throughout the empire will hear what the queen did and will start talking to their husbands the same way. There will be no end to the contempt and anger throughout your realm. [19] So if it please the king, we suggest that you issue a written decree, a law of the Persians and Medes that cannot be revoked. It should order that Queen Vashti be forever banished from your presence and that you choose another queen more worthy than she.

My God, this was an awesome verdict. What really happened? Disobedience moved her out of position and the door was open up for someone else to pursue their destiny. They all said that women would disrespect their husbands again regardless of their rank or position in life. This made good sense to the king and letters were sent to all parts of the kingdom.

What a tremendous revelation, to understand that we can abort our destinies though disobedience and God will raise someone else up to take our place.

God has a plan for our lives and no one can abort it but us. God has a goal for our lives and no one can abort it but us. He's already shown us what He can do. He's shown us he can make a way out of no way. He's shown us he can open many doors that have been closed. Sometimes I don't understand Him or understand what He wants me to do. But, I'm going to keep on trusting Him. I'm going to keep on leaning and depending on Him. I'm going to keep on standing on His word. We are no different from Queen Vashti. She made a mistake. She may have listened to the wrong advice. She may have been deceived by Satan, but whatever the reason, it cost her. It cost her status. It cost her position. It cost her fame. It cost her money. It may have cost her the throne. And it may have cost her life. That's what the devil wants you to do. He wants you to forget that God can raise someone else up in your place. He wants you to forget that you aren't all that. He wants you to forget you are dispensable. He's trying to get your disobedience to abort your destiny!

CHAPTER FOUR

JUST ONE NIGHT WITH THE KING

When the turn came for Esther (the girl Mordecai had adopted, the daughter of his uncle Abihail) to go to the king, she asked for nothing other than what Hegai, the king's eunuch who was in charge of the harem, suggested. And Esther won the favor of everyone who saw her. She was taken to King Xerxes in the royal residence in the tenth month, the month of Tebeth, in the seventh year of his reign. Now the king was attracted to Esther more than to any of the other women, and she won his favor and approval more than any of the other virgins. So he set a royal crown on her head and made her queen instead of Vashti. Esther 2:15-17

There was a farm girl on the distant horizon that the King was about to elevate. She was a peasant and she was a poor girl. She was considered a nobody. There are some people reading this today that God is about to elevate. He's getting ready to take some failures and make them successes. He's getting ready to take some nobodies and make them some-bodies. He's getting ready to take some Haddeshs and make them Queen Esthers. This is exactly what happens in Esther's life, but she had to prepare for her opportunity, which was just one night with the King.

You must have the basic ingredients.

Now after the King had gotten over having his ego bruised and losing his relationship with his wife, the text says that he appointed officers in all of the providences of his kingdom to search for beautiful young virgins to bring unto the palace Shushan and the place them under the care of Hegai his chamberlain, the keeper of the women to begin the purification process. You see, none of the young girls could enter into his presence until they had been purified.

We likewise must remain pure to continue to enter into God's presence; otherwise, we are just fooling ourselves and playing church instead of being empowered by the Holy Spirit. Maybe the reason so many Christians today are defeated is because they think they can approach the presence of God just any kind of way without sincerity and pureness of heart.

In the palace was a Jewish officer by the name of Mordecai. He brought in his cousin by the name of Hadassah, also known as Esther to the palace and she was fine. Chapter 2:7 says Mordecai had a cousin named Hadassah, whom he had brought up because she had neither father nor mother. This girl, who was also known as Ester, was lovely in form and features, and Mordecai had taken her as his own daughter when her father and mother died.

The basic ingredients were that these girls had to be virgins, young and fine.

If we are going to get the favor of God in our lives there are some basic ingredients we must have.

We must be born again. Our hearts must be pure of sin as a virgin is clean from the stains of sexual sin. We must be young in heart. We must have a teachable spirit, not thinking that we know it all. If we are going to get the favor of God, we must be anointed and know what we have been anointed for. We must know the Word and how to stand on this Word, using our faith rather than giving up at every difficult point in our lives. That's basic stuff.

You must have favor with those who serve the king.

If you are going to reach your destiny and obtain the favor of God, you cannot by-pass the people who God has placed in your life to help you prepare to meet the king. Neither can you say that I don't need anybody to help me. That's not gospel according to His word. Hegai, the chamberlain could have aborted Esther's dreams before she ever got an audience with the King. But instead of cutting her off, he assisted her. Notice verses 8, 9 Ester 2:8-9.

When the king's order and edict had been proclaimed, many girls were brought to the citadel of Susa and put under the care of Hegai. Esther also was taken to the king's palace and entrusted to Hegai, who had charge of the harem. [9] The girl pleased him and won his favor. Immediately he provided her with her beauty treatments and special food. He assigned her seven maids selected form the king's palace and moved her and her maids into the best place in the harem.

God has placed Hegai(s) and chamberlains in our lives to prepare us for our day of opportunity. Ephesians 4:11 says, And he gave some, apostles; and some, prophets; and some, evangelists; and some, pastors and teachers; for the perfecting of the saints, for the work of the ministry, for the edifying of the body of Christ: [13] till we all come in the unity of the faith, and of the knowledge of the Son of God, unto a perfect man, unto the measure of the stature of the fullness of Christ.

Your pastor, co-pastor, overseer, bishop or some other leader could be the very one that God has sent into your life to help you to get ready for your night with the King.

You Must Be Prepared for Your Opportunity (You must be prepared to meet the king.)

Now none of these young virgins stood a chance without first qualifying. To qualify for an audience with the king, they had to go through 12 months of purification.

Esther 2:12 says, Before a girl's turn came to go into the King Xerxes, she had to complete twelve months of beauty treatments prescribed for the women, six months with oil of myrrh and six with perfumes and cosmetics.

You see in 12 months if any of the girls had been lying about being virgins it would have shown up. When we go through extensive periods of purification before we are elevated, if there are any impurities in us, they are going to show up. They had to go through six months of preparation with oil of myrrh. Myrrh was bitter oil. Myrrh was used for anointing, for women's purification and many other uses. Along with myrrh, the text says sweet odors, meaning perfumes and cosmetics. It was the bating and mixing of bitter and sweet oils that gave Esther, her unique smell.

It is the bathing and soaking in the Holy Spirit that prepares us. It is the mixing of bitter trials and tribulations with sweet oils of praise and worship that gives us our unique smell and anointing. You see this smell is not for us, but it's for God. God wants to be able to smell our praise and worship as we go through the trial and tribulations of preparation. God wants us to come out with an anointing that's been smeared and rubbed into our very existence.

You must take advantage of the advice that comes from the king's servants.

The strongest point in this lesson is what made Esther ready for just one night with the King. It was that she took the advice of Hegai. Hegai had been with the king. Hegai knew what the king liked and disliked.

When the turn came for Esther (the girl Mordecai had adopted, the daughter of his uncle Abihail) to go to the king, **she asked for nothing** other than what Hegai, the king's eunuch who was in charge of the harem, **suggested.** And Esther won the favor of everyone who saw her.

And Esther obtained favour in the sight of all them that looked upon her. God has given us Hegai(s), spiritual mentors and fathers who can hint to us on how to approach the King and what kind of conversation we should hold with the King, what the King likes and dislikes, what he eats and doesn't eat, how the king dresses and doesn't dress, what the kings' favorite colors are, what the king's favorite foods are. When it comes to the King of Kings, who is Jesus, we need to get advice from a chamberlain, a pastor or spiritual mentor who has been into the secret place of the Lord who can help prepare us for our one night with the Lord. And when our opportunity for favor comes, we can say that we have been prepared to meet the king.

Now there were four important points that our text brought out on our way to restoration and blessings from the King. Esther discovered them to be:

Main points of the chapter:

1. **You must have the basic ingredients** — for us that means personal relationship with God . . .

2. **You must have favor with those who serve the king** — Understand the purpose for spiritual leaders

in your life and demonstrate appreciation and respect for them . . .

3. **You must be prepared for your opportunity** — You must be prepared to meet the king and be willing to go through the process . . .

4. **You must take advantage of the advice that comes from the king's servants** — You should glean from others who have gone before you who are committed to God.

All it takes is just one night with the Lord and your life will never be the same again. Take whatever trouble you've got to take. Put up with whatever you must put up with. Take orders from whom you must take orders from. Listen to whom you must listen to. Go through whatever spiritual boot camp you need to go through and just one night with the king will change your entire destiny.

And so Esther was taken into the King Xerxes royal house in the tenth month and seventh year of his reign and verse 17 says, "And the king loved Esther above all the women, and she obtained grace and favour in his sight more than all the virgins; so that he set the royal crown upon her head, and made her queen instead of Vashti.

There will come a time when you will be presented with an opportunity in your life for blessings and prosperity, but favor can only be realized when you have made all of the necessary preparations.

True favor is not favoritism, but it is when preparation meets opportunity.

Favoritism is being exalted before your season. Favoritism will get you in trouble with God. Favoritism is not remaining humble. Favoritism will cause you to give up when difficulties arise, but true favor comes only after preparation has taken place.

Some of you may be asking the question, why hasn't my life been filled with more favor? Could it be that you are not taking advantage of the small opportunities of life and you are not preparing yourself to meet the king? Could it be that you're still making excuses for allowing someone else to get ahead of you? Could it be that you're not fighting the good fight of faith and you're engaged in flesh fights or carnality instead? No one should determine your destiny but God. Not even you should get in the way of Him when it comes to your destiny. What God has for you it is for you, if you don't abort it!

You should be saying to yourself right now, all I need is just one night with the King. All I need is just one extraordinary encounter with God, and my life will never be the same. All I need is just one intimate encounter with God, and my life will never be the same. All I need is to stop accusing others for my failures, and get myself together, and my life will never be the same again.

Sometimes the king represents the person(s) in our lives that God uses to give us favor. So have you prepared yourself for the home loan? Have you prepared yourself for the college degree? Have you prepared yourself for the contract?

The decision to bless you for the rest of your life is going to be made in just one night. Are you ready to be blessed? Are you ready to be elevated?

Are you ready to be promoted? Are you ready to go to the next level? Get it together!

It was at night that Jacob wrestled with God . . . It was at night that God delivered the Children of Israel from Egypt. It was at night in a vision when Daniel received his revelation. It was at night when the Shepherds saw the star of David about the manger. It was at night that God shook the prison door and freed Paul and Silas. All it takes is just one night with the Lord and your life will never be the same again!

CHAPTER FIVE

YOU DON'T HAVE TO START OUT GREAT TO END UP GREAT

And Gideon said unto him, Oh my Lord, if the LORD be with us, why then is all this befallen us? And where be all his miracles which our fathers told us of, saying, Did not the LORD bring us up from Egypt? But now the LORD hath forsaken us, and delivered us into the hands of the Midianites. And the LORD looked upon him, and said, Go in this thy might, and thou shalt save Israel from the hand of the Midianites: have not I sent thee? And he said unto him, Oh my Lord, wherewith shall I save Israel? Behold, my family is poor in Manasseh, and I am the least in my father's house. And the LORD said unto him, Surely, I will be with thee, and thou shalt smite the Midianites as one man.
Judges 6:13-16

So Gideon, and the hundred men that were with him, came unto the outside of the camp in the beginning of the middle watch; and they had but newly set the watch: and they blew the trumpets, and brake the pitchers that were in their hands. And the three companies blew the trumpets, and brake the pitchers, and held the lamps in their left hands, and the trumpets in their right hands to blow withal: and they cried, The sword of the LORD, and of Gideon. And they stood every man in his place round about the camp: and all the host ran, and cried, and fled.
Judges 7:19-21

The lamps in their left hands, and the trumpets in their right hands to blow withal: and they cried, the sword of the Lord, and of Gideon. [21] And they stood every man in his place round about the camp: and all the host ran, and cried and fled.

God has not forsaken us.

Let us not make any mistake as we read this chapter about feeling defeated at times. Sometimes we even feel conquered and overthrown. It is not that God has forsaken us, but it is normally because we have forsaken God. It is because we have forgotten about the importance of our relationship with God, and we began to establish relationships and covenants outside of the will of God. Israel, under the leadership of Joshua made tremendous progress possessing the territory that God had instructed them to conquer, however; it was the people whom they failed to destroy that later on caused them to backslide on God. When God tells you to do away with a thing it is because God knows that thing will come back to haunt you. After the death of Joshua, Israel falls away from the purpose and plan of God over and over. God continually raises up one Judge after another to deliver Israel's enemies. At this point, we see Israel under the oppression of the Midianites. For seven years Midian oppressed Israel. The Midianites were so cruel that they made the children of Israel run and hide themselves in caves and dens. The raiders would come upon the fields and crops and destroy all, leaving Israel with no food. All of the sheep, oxen and donkeys would be confiscated and Israel would be left to starve to death.

Often we reap what we sow.

Israel was reduced to literal starvation and they began to cry out unto the Lord. The Lord sent them a prophet. The prophet told them that God said that He had brought them out of Egyptian bondage. He led them across the Red Sea. He took them through the wilderness and allowed them to conquer their enemies who were already lodging in the promise land. But they backslid and began to worship the Amorites God. If you are under a lot of pressure today, know that God is going to show you some things about yourself before He delivers you. He is going to show you that often we reap what we sow.

Nevertheless, God still answers prayers and God will give us an answer and a plan for our deliverance. The bible says, "Then the angel of the Lord came and sat beneath the oak tree at Ophrah, which belonged to Joash of the clan of Abiezer. Gideon son of Joash had been threshing wheat at the bottom of a winepress to hide grain to hide the grain form the Midianites. [12] The angel of the Lord appeared to him and said, "Mighty hero, the Lord is with you!"

[13] "Sir," Gideon replied, "if the Lord is with us, why has all this happened to us? And where are all the miracles our ancestors told us about? Didn't they say, 'The Lord brought us up out of Egypt?' But now the Lord has abandoned us and handed us over to the Midianites." [NLT] We often reap what we sow. And the sooner we stop blaming others for our troubles, the sooner we are on the road to recovery. The sooner we repent and change our ways, the sooner God will deliver us and give us victory over our enemies. Get yourself together and watch God begin to work on your behalf.

**We Can't Make Excuses;
It's Not About Us.**

Actually the Lord had not abandoned Israel but Israel had abandoned the Lord for idol Gods. Immediately the Lord calls Gideon. The Lord tells Gideon, go mighty man and deliver your people, I'm sending you. You will defeat the Midianites as if you were fighting one man. But Gideon, like many of us began to make all kinds of excuses why he could not go. Gideon said that His clan was the weakest in the tribe of Manessah, and he was the least in his entire family. We can't make excuses because it's not about us. It's about what God is getting ready to do through us. It's not about our power and might, but it's by His Spirit saith the Lord. The way to experience God in your life is not about creating your own agenda and asking God to join you at work, but it's about finding out what He's doing in the earth and joining Him at work. In this case all Gideon needed to do was hush his mouth and follow God's commands without back talk. In many cases, all we need to do is follow God's commands and keep our mouths closed.

God Uses Zeros

Gideon didn't realize that he was an ideal candidate for the job, because God specializes in hiring zeros. God calls the least likely candidate from one's point of view to do the miraculous. God will not share his glory with the proud and self sufficient. After God reveals himself unto Gideon through confirmation, God tells Gideon to destroy the items of idolatry and the false God Baal. God using zeros is a pattern all throughout scripture. We ought to be thankful today for this biblical pattern, because if it had not been for the Lord on our side, where would we be. I'm personally glad about this revelation, because I wouldn't be where I am today, if God hadn't used this zero.

Gideon Fleeces The Lord

Then *Gideon fleeces* the Lord.

Judges 6:36-40

Then Gideon said to God, "If you are truly going to use me to rescue Israel as you promised, [37] prove it to me in this way. I will put some wool on the threshing floor tonight. If the **fleece is wet** with dew in the morning **but the ground is dry,** then I will know that you are going to help me rescue Israel as you promised." [38] And it happened just that way. When Gideon got up the next morning, he squeezed the fleece and wrung out a whole bowlful of water. [39] Then Gideon said to God, "Please don't be angry with me, but let me make one more request. This time let **the fleece remain dry** while the **ground around it is wet** with dew." [40] so that night God did as Gideon asked. The fleece was dry in the morning, but the ground was covered with dew . . . Gideon fleeced the Lord and the Lord honored his request, but always remember the Lord is not obligated to prove himself to any man. He is God all by himself. If he honors your fleecing request, it is simply because He loves you so much that He is willing to go the extra mile with you to get you to the right place in Him.

Your Greatness Is Not In Your Numbers

Even after we decide to finally be obedient unto God's

47

command, he's not going to give us victory because of our strength or numbers. He will reduce us to a level that only He will get the glory from. The bible says that Gideon gathered together 32,000 men to fight against 135,000 Midianites. The Israelites were already outnumbered 4 to 1, but God said that was too many. All of the fearful ones which was 22,000, God sent them home which left 10,000; but God said that was too much. Any time that God raises the level of commitment, faithfulness and loyalty it will always separate the boys from the men. So after all who are fearful are removed, God removes the non vigilant. Only 300 men lapped water from the stream like dogs while the 9,700 put their faces into the water and forgot about being watchful. You must always remember that we must watch and pray. We must remain conscientious that there's still an enemy who's seeking to devour us. Our greatness is not in numbers. 300 is a good number. 300 represents faithfulness. 300 represents loyalty. 300 represents commitment. To overcome the enemy all you need is faithfulness, loyalty, and commitment.

The main point of this chapter was to reveal unto the body of Christ that greatness comes through passionate worship. Our greatness is not dependent upon our last name or what side of the tracks we were born on. Our greatness is also not dependent upon our resources or our numbers, but our victory depends upon our ability to worship God.

We can make all the excuses that we want to make but God made us to be great. Our greatness is not in what family we were born into. Being born on the wrong side of the tracks is no excuse for not being somebody. It's not an excuse for not excelling. We are somebody because He has made us and called us before we entered into our mother's womb.

He knew our capabilities since eternity pass.

We can even delay the process by fleecing God, but that will not ultimately affect what God has in store for us.

Even having limited resources can not affect us, because God is use to taking little to become much. He reduced Gideon down to three hundred men. He even gave him a dream with the interpretation thereof insuring Him of victory.

And then finally, God showed Gideon, that his victory was ultimately in how well he could worship. He told Gideon to take the men down to the enemy's camp and blow their horns and break their jars. At about midnight Gideon and his men began to break the jars and blow the horns. They put a sword in one hand and a torch in the other and shouted a **sword for the Lord** and a **sword for Gideon**. And God will help them to fight their battles. And God will help us fight our battles too.

But the victory and greatness came through the worship. The enemy was confused and each man began to turn on one another. If you praise and worship your God today, He will make your enemies your footstool. He will make your enemies throw down their weapons. He will make your enemies be in confusion. He will make your enemies be in disarray. I'm glad to know a God who will fight for me. I'm glad to know that the Lord is on my side because I'm on His side.

You don't have to start out great to end up great. There is no need to make excuses. There is no need to complain about your family. There is no need to complain about your ability. The truth of the matter is that there's greatness inside of you. There's ability inside of you. There's creativity inside of you. There are solutions inside of you and you don't have to fleece him. You don't have to doubt him.

Just remember, ultimate greatness belongs to worshippers! Are you a worshipper? If you are, you ought to praise him always like you are losing your mind!

CHAPTER SIX

DON'T DESPISE SMALL BEGINNINGS

And Joseph was brought down to Egypt; and Potiphar, an officer of Pharaoh, captain of the guard, an Egyptian, bought him of the hands of the Ishmeelites, which had brought him down thither. And the LORD was with Joseph, and he was a prosperous man; and he was in the house of his master the Egyptian. And his master saw that the LORD was with him, and that the LORD made all that he did to prosper in his hand. And Joseph found grace in his sight, and he served him: and he made him overseer over his house, and all that he had he put into his hand. And it came to pass from the time that he had made him overseer in his house, and over all that he had, that the LORD blessed the Egyptian's house for Joseph's sake; and the blessing of the LORD was upon all that he had in the house, and in the field. And he left all that he had in Joseph's hand; and he knew not ought he had, save the read which he did eat. And Joseph was a goodly person, and well favoured.
Genesis 39:1-6

The believer must see that every opportunity is a prelude to something very great that is about to happen in their lives. He or she should not despise small beginnings because it may be the beginning of something very awesome that is about to occur.

Oftentimes we don't take small opportunities seriously but they are the ones that God watches to see what our attitudes and responses will be. Therefore we cannot take them lightly but take full advantage of every opportunity for the glory of God.

We Are Destined for Greatness, but we must be proactive rather than reactive. The prefix pro-means before activity... So we are responsible for planning the outcome of our lives. We must be responsible. We have the ability to choose the correct response. However reactive people are people, who allow other people or circumstances, to determine their destinies. Reactive people are affected by their environment. They go through life reacting to what others have planned. Proactive or responsible people can create their own environment in spite of their surroundings.

Life is full of setbacks and disappointments, but we cannot allow them to deter us from accomplishing our dreams and goals. The devil's job is to put up as much resistance as he possibly can to keep us from our destiny, but we must preserve, pray always and faint not; never, never give up!

So next to being responsible or proactive is that we must see where we want to be. **Isaiah 46: 9-10**, tells us, "Remember the former things of old: for I am God, and there is none else; I am God, and there is none like me, [10] Declaring the end from the beginning, and from ancient times the things that are not yet done, saying, My counsel shall stand, and I will do all my pleasure:" Notice **Romans 4:16-17**, "Therefore it is of faith, that it might be by grace; to the end the promise might be sure to all the seed; not to that only which is of the law, but to that also which is of the faith of Abraham; who is the father of us all, [17] (As it is written, I have made thee a father of many nations,) before him whom he believed, even God, who quickeneth the dead, and calleth those things which be not as though they were. " If God Himself saw where He wanted to be, we also must see where we want to be and began to speak (calleth) some things into existence by faith.

Notice this brief point in (Genesis 37:3-4) Now Israel loved Joseph more than all his children,
JOSEPH RECEIVED FAVOR...
IT'S THE FATHERS PEROGATIVE TO DO AS HE PLEASES WITH WHAT'S HIS...
Because he was the son of his old age: and he made him a coat of many colors,
JOSEPH RECEIVED RECOGNITION...

WHEN FAVOR IS UPON YOUR LIFE, OTHERS CAN'T HELP BUT RECOGNIZE...

[4] And when his brethren saw that their father loved him _(favored him)_ more than all his brethren, they hated him, and could not speak peaceably unto him.

WHEN THE FATHER'S FAVOR IS UPON YOU
EXPECT TO BE HATED BY YOUR BROTHERS...

1.   DON'T ALLOW HATERS TO KILL YOUR DESTINY
Notice: Genesis 39:1-6 And Joseph was brought down to Egypt; and Potiphar, an officer of Pharaoh, captain of the guard, an Egyptian, brought him of the hands of the Ishmaelite, which brought him down thither. [2] And the Lord was with Joseph, and he was a prosperous man; and

he was in the house of his master the Egyptian.

2. YOU HAVE TO KNOW WHEN THE LORD IS WITH YOU

[3] And his master saw that the Lord was with him, and that the Lord made all that he did to prosper in his hand.

3. EVERYTHING YOU TOUCH, THE LORD WILL BLESS WHEN HE IS WITH YOU

[4] And Joseph found grace *(favor)* in his sight, and he served him: and he made him overseer over his house, and all that he had he put into his hand. [5] And it came to pass from the time that he had made him overseer in his house, and over all that he had, that the Lord blessed the Egyptian's house for Joseph's sake; and the blessing of the Lord was upon all that he had in the house, and in the field.

4. GOD WILL MAKE YOUR BOSS LOOK GOOD BECAUSE OF YOU

[6] And he left all that he had in Joseph's hand; and he knew not ought he had, save the bread which he did eat. And Joseph was a goodly person, and well *favoured.* [KJV]

5. YOU WILL NOT HAVE TO LIVE BY A BUDGET WHEN GOD BLESSES YOU BEYOND MEASURE

Notice this reference in Luke 16:1-12. Here in this story Jesus gives His disciples the story about a rich man that left his business in the hands of a manager or steward that had wasted his money. And the owner said, what's this I hear about my money is? Vs 1, 2

This put the manager in a panic and he was quite concerned about his job. Vs 3

All of a sudden he gets the bright idea about what to do. He says I'm going to call everybody that owes my boss and see what I can get from them

[5] So he called every one of his lord's debtors unto him,

and said unto the first, How much owest thou unto my lord? [6] And he said, An hundred measures of oil. And he said unto him, Take thy bill, and sit down quickly, and write fifty. [7] Then said he to another, And how much owest thou? And he said, An hundred measures of wheat. And he said unto him, Take thy bill, and write fourscore. [8] And the lord commended the unjust steward, because he had done wisely: for the children of this world are in their generation wiser than the children of light. [9] And I say unto you, Make to yourselves friends of the mammon (world) of unrighteousness; that, when ye fail, they may receive you into everlasting habitations. [10] He that is faithful in that which is least is faithful also in much: and he that is unjust in the least is unjust also in much. [11] If therefore ye have not been faithful in the unrighteous mammon, who will commit to your trust the true riches? [12] And if ye have not been faithful in that which is another man's, who shall give you that which is your own?

6. LEARN TO BE FAITHFUL IN THAT WHICH IS ANOTHER MAN'S

TAKE ADVANTAGE OF EVERY OPPORTUNITY THAT GOD LEADS YOU INTO WHETHER GREAT OR SMALL...
And don't forget to ask the Lord for wisdom in everything...
Don't Despise small beginnings. God specializes in taking nothing and making something; he specializes in taking nobodies and making them some bodies; He specializes in taking a little bit and making a whole lot; He's a just and awesome God. And I want to encourage everyone reading this chapter to not give up on your dreams no matter what other people are saying. You are in control of your destiny.

No one can abort the great future that God has predestined for you but you. So go on and let the player haters talk; Go on and allow them to run their mouths, but you practice the golden rule, which is, do unto others as you would have them to do unto you and God will ensure that blessings keep coming your way.

My brothers and sisters, I'm not where I want to be, but thanks be to God that I'm not where I use to be. The Lord has been good to me. Abundant Life International Baptist Church didn't start out as an international ministry. We started out as Concerned Christians for A Better Sandy Run Church. We were not even local. As a matter of fact we were just a bunch of nobodies trying to tell everybody about somebody who could save anybody. We just love the Lord and He heard our cry and delivered us and every since that day, we have been not despising small beginnings. What's coming is greater than what's been and God is just beginning. Really, He's just beginning to bless all of us. So don't despise small beginnings.

Learn to be faithful in another man's. Know that the Lord is with you. Keep touching stuff because God is going to bless it. DON'T DESPISE SMALL BEGINNINGS.

CHAPTER SEVEN

LOOKING AT LIFE FROM GOD'S POINT OF VIEW

When Joseph's brothers saw that their father was dead, they said, "What if Joseph holds a grudge against us and pays us back for all the wrongs we did to him?" So they sent word to Joseph, saying, "Your father left these instructions before he died: This is what you are to say to Joseph: I ask you to forgive your brothers the sins and the wrongs they committed in treating you so badly.' Now please forgive the sins of the servants of the God of your father." When their message came to him, Joseph wept. His brothers then came and threw themselves down before him. "We are your slaves," they said. But Joseph said to them, "Don't be afraid. Am I in the place of God? You intended to harm me, but God intended it for good to accomplish what is now being done, the saving of many lives. So then, don't be afraid. I will provide for you and your children." And he reassured them and spoke kindly to them.
Genesis 50:15-21

When Joseph's brethren saw that their father was dead, they said, Joseph will peradventure hate us, and will certainly requite us all the evil which we did unto him. [16] And they sent a messenger unto Joseph, saying, Thy father did command before he died, saying, [17] So shall ye say unto Joseph, Forgive, I pray thee now, the trespass of thy brethren, and their sin; for they did unto thee evil: and now, we pray thee, forgive the trespass of the servants of the God of thy father. And Joseph wept when they spake unto him. [18] And his brethren also went and fell down before his face; and they said, Behold, we be thy servants. [19] And Joseph said unto them, Fear not: for am I in the place of God? [20] But as for you, ye thought evil against me; but God meant it unto good, to bring to pass, as it is this day, to save much people alive. [21] Now therefore fear ye not: I will nourish you, and your little ones. And he comforted them, and spake kindly unto them.

Every negative situation in life has the potential to take us out, but it also has the potential to bless us without measure.

Regardless of what we go through in life, what is more important than what we go through; is how we handle what we go through. We must get to the place that we can see the positive aspect or (silver lining) in every dark cloud, the potential out of every disaster, and the positive out of every negative. We must get to the place that we are looking at life from God's point of view.

God does not define persons and things in the present tense, but He defines everything by its future tense. He does not see us as we are, but He sees us, as we shall become.

When Joseph was thrown into the pit by his brothers, God did not see a slave but God saw a prince. God had a different point of view.

God knew that at some point, Joseph would discover himself and begin to use his God given talent and ability to prosper him and bring him into greatness.

You are destined for greatness today also and no matter where you are right now, began to look at life from God's point of view.

This chapter will give us a clearer understanding of his Godly principle of having the right perspective on life.
In this story, Joseph's father dies and his brothers are now afraid that he will take their lives. They think that their only chance of survival is to mention their father's last request to ask Joseph to forgive them of their evil deeds. And so Joseph's brothers fall down in humble submission at his feet and this turned the tide three hundred and sixty degrees. They thought they had power over Joseph's life, but Joseph had the real power over their lives. Joseph had the opportunity at this point to truly humiliate them but instead he spares them and says that he's not God over them.

But As For You, Ye Thought Evil Against Me;

Joseph tells his brothers that they did him wrong by attempting to take his life and eventually selling him into slavery. The course of Joseph's life was supposed to end quickly and in a tragic manner according to his brothers' plan. The wicked one, called Satan had placed this diabolical plan in the mind of these brothers, because he had peeped into the future and saw Joseph blessed and others as well.

Throughout our lives, there have been persons, including family members who have done us wrong at certain times in our lives. The thoughts that Satan had placed in the minds of some people concerning us were detrimental and designed to bring about our demise and destruction. The

59

truth is that many of us believers have been physically, sexually and mentally abused by family members. Uncle Buds and Auntie Mays have taken little nieces and nephews in secluded places of iniquity and had their pleasures fulfilled. Some of the horrendous things that they did unto us during our youth should have devastated our futures but God intervened into our lives at the right moment and prevented some of us from committing even suicide.

Satan wants to destroy us because he has peeped into our futures and he has seen the blessings that God has in store for us. He will use any tool or device he can to abort our destinies, but God sees things from a different point of view and it is God's point of view that we need to acquire. (Verse 20a)

But God Meant It For Good

Joseph eloquently tells his brothers that God had other objectives concerning their actions. God has an uncanny way of setting us up for our blessings. Could this be to psych the devil out, making him assume that he is getting the advantage of us, only to turn the tables at the last moment?

Two writers in the bible allude to this practice by God in their scriptural comments. Listen to what James has to say in the first chapter verses 2-4, "My brethren, count it all joy when ye fall into divers temptations; [3] Knowing this, that the trying of your faith worketh patience. [4] But let patience have her perfect work, that ye may be perfect and entire, wanting nothing.

James says that all of the negative stuff in our lives can be reversed and tallied up to equal a positive integer or numeral in our lives. In addition, the Apostle Paul gives us one of the most famous quotes in the bible in the book of Romans that again reveals God's unusual way of setting us up for our blessings. This is how the Apostle puts it in Romans 8:28 "And we know that all things work together for good to them that love God, to them who are called according to his purpose." Therefore, when we cannot see anything positive in our negative situations, there is a God who is working behind the scenes orchestrating a masterpiece on our behalf?

Our lives are like lumps of clay in the potter's hands without form or fashion. The process to becoming something beautiful and useful is messy and ugly, but through meticulous manipulation by the master potter, the clay evolves into a beautiful piece of artwork. It is through meticulous manipulation that God makes us great and successful in his life regardless of the numerous misfortunes and deliberate plots of destruction by our enemies.

We love the Lord. Moreover, we have been called according to his purpose. Therefore, many negative situations are working toward our good because God is working toward our good in the situation.

In sickness, He is working toward our good. In poverty, He is working toward our good. In abusive situations, He is working toward our good. When we have money, he is working toward our good and when we do not have money, he is working toward our good. You have to know, that God's promises is true to never leave us or forsake us.

These are just a few examples of him working toward our good. (Verse 20b) The key to coming out successful is looking at life from God's point of view.

To Save Much People Alive

Joseph had come to realize what his purpose in life was and he had come to understand God's methodology in preparing him for his destiny.

Joseph had the ability to endure hardship but that was not his purpose. Joseph was an excellent planner and prognosticator but that was not his purpose. Joseph was an excellent dreamer and visionary but that was not his purpose. Joseph had the uncanny ability to interpret dreams as well and that was not his purpose, but Joseph's purpose was very much like ours, to bless God and others in this life with the gifts and talents that God has endowed unto us.
We must come to realize our purposes in life and understand God's methodology in preparing us for our destinies. Things are not always the way that they appear. Sometimes we may think that our lives are complete tragedies but in the background God is working things out. He has one major goal in mind, that our lives would be productive and prosperous, but most importantly, a blessing to other people. You are the designers original. You can do what no other person on the planet can do. You only need to discover who God is and whom He has made you to be. Change your perception of life. Learn to take the bitter with the sweet, because God is working in all situations. He is working on your behalf to bring you out unscathed.

As I bring this powerful chapter to a close, and after all the hell Joseph's brothers put him through; He is still concerned about them. Most of us would have wanted revenge, but Joseph says in verse twenty-one, "Now therefore fear ye not: I will nourish you, and your little ones. And he comforted them, and spake kindly unto them. Joseph had the power to send his brothers to their graves, but instead he feeds them and their families. He becomes a provider and protector for the ones who tried to destroy him from the face of the earth.

(My) Brothers and sisters, we have to change our way of thinking. We have to understand that if God (be) for us, who can be against us? What individuals meant for evil, God meant it for our good. What abusers and users meant for evil, God meant for our good.

I want to personally thank every person who did me wrong. Everyone who lied on me, I want to thank you. Everyone who talked about me, I want to thank you. Everyone who ever ran me down, I want to thank you. Everyone who ever used me, I want to thank you. Everyone who ever tried to hold me back, I want to thank you.
You ought to thank everyone who ever tried to destroy you and failed, because they made you who you are today. They didn't realize it but God was using them to set you up for your blessing.

Moses would have never been great if it had not been for Pharaoh. David would have never been great if it had not been for Goliath. Muhammad Ali would have never been great if it had not been for Joe Frazier. The Green Bay Packers would have never been great if it had not been for the Dallas Cowboys.

You need to start looking at life from God's point of view.

Start asking this question; how can God turn this situation around for my good; about every negative thing that has come into your life. Ask yourself what lifelong lesson or principle is God trying to convey unto me from this experience?

Remember as long as you live there will be haters who are trying to abort your destiny, but you are destined for greatness. But, God is always trying to do you good when others are trying to do you in. Every set back can be turned into a set up for wonderful things to come into your life. And ultimately, what God wants to do is to use you to bless others, including those who have been your enemies.

So, don't let the haters get under your skin. Bless them and curse them not. Look at life from God's point of view.
If you have been allowing the enemy to get you down and cause you to lose your drive towards your destiny, you ought to allow Jesus to impact your thinking by looking at life from God's point of view.

CHAPTER EIGHT

PROBLEM SOLVERS AND NOT PROBLEM MAKERS

Then Pharaoh said to Joseph, "Inasmuch as God has shown you all this, there is no one as discerning and wise as you. 40 You shall be over my house, and all my people shall be ruled according to your word; only in regard to the throne will I be greater than you." 41 And Pharaoh said to Joseph, "See, I have set you over all the land of Egypt."
42 Then Pharaoh took his signet ring off his hand and put it on Joseph's hand; and he clothed him in garments of fine linen and put a gold chain around his neck. 43 And he had him ride in the second chariot which he had; and they cried out before him, "Bow the knee!" So he set him over all the land of Egypt.
Genesis 41:39-43

True prosperity and success really comes into our lives when we allow God to use us to bring healings and blessings to a hurting world. You were placed on this earth to be a problem solver and not a problem maker. The happiest people in our society are people who are blessing others with their gifts and talents. The most-unhappy people in the world are those who are not making significant contributions to the world, but instead are creating pain and destruction for the rest of us.

Every inventor of the ages set out with one major goal in mind and that was to solve a problem. Thomas Edison solved the problem of having no lights at night by creating the light bulb. Mr. Bell eliminated the cross country communication problem by creating the telegraph/telephone system. Mr. Henry Ford eliminated the land transportation problem by building the very reliable Model T motorcar. And, the Wright Brothers eliminated the problem of flight by being the first to fly. Successful people are problem solvers and not problem makers.

To be successful in this life God has given all of us the ability to {find a need and fulfill it}. This is how you become great! Finding a need and fulfilling it!

YOU HAVE BEEN CALLED TO SOLVE A PROBLEM...

Do something about your dreams and visions

The background story in this chapter shows us how God gives us dreams, visions and revelations for the express purpose of doing something about them. It is the dreamer's responsibility to make application and implementation of what God has disclosed unto them. It shows us how we have been called to solve a problem.

Study Genesis 41:25-32

And Joseph said unto Pharaoh, The dream of Pharaoh is one: God hath shewed Pharaoh what he is about to do. [26] The seven good kine (good cows) are seven years; and the seven good ears (heads of grain) are seven years: the dream is one. [27] And the seven thin and ill favoured kine (skinny ugly cows) that came up after them are seven years; and the seven empty ears (worthless heads) blasted with the east wind shall be seven; years of famine. [28] This is the thing which I have spoken unto Pharaoh: What God is about to do he sheweth unto Pharaoh.

[29] Behold, there come seven years of great plenty throughout all the land of Egypt: [30] And there shall arise after them seven years of famine; and all the plenty shall be forgotten in the land of Egypt; and the famine shall consume the land [31] And the plenty shall not be known in the land by reason of that famine following; for it shall be very grievous. [32] And for that the dream was doubled unto Pharaoh twice; it is because the thing is established by God, and God will shortly bring it to pass.

- IF GOD KEEPS BRINGING SOMETHING BACK TO YOU, IT'S PROPHETIC IN NATURE...

Genesis 41:33-52 Now therefore let Pharaoh look out a man discreet and wise, and set him over the land of Egypt. JOSEPH HAS THE PLAN, HE HAS THE SOLUTION TO THE PROBLEM BUT NOTICE HE NEVER EXALTS HIMSELF...

- He doesn't tell Pharaoh how to do his job...
- He knows his place and stays within it...
- We could accomplish more if we stayed in our lane and ran our own race...

[34]Let Pharaoh do this, and let him appoint officers over the land, and take up the fifth part of the land of Egypt in the seven plenteous years.

[35]And let them gather all the food of those good year that

come, and lay up corn under the hand of Pharaoh, and let them keep food in the cities.

[36]And that food shall be for store to the land against the seven years of famine, which shall be in the land of Egypt; that the land perish not through the famine.

[37]And the thing was good in the eyes of Pharaoh, and in the eyes of all his servants.

[38]And Pharaoh said unto his servants, Can we find such a one as this is, a man in whom the Spirit of God is?

EVEN PHARAOH RECOGNIZES THAT THIS ANSWER WAS SENT FROM GOD...

If you can get someone on your team who allows God to give the answers, then you can be a sure winner...

Pharaoh's dream of seven years of plenty and seven years of famine had been interpreted by Joseph... And our story shows us how God can take us from rags to riches when we allow Him to give us the solution to problems.

...God hath shewed thee all this,

In Genesis 41:39, God had given the revelation unto Joseph. He showed Joseph what was about to occur because He wanted to use Joseph. And not only did God want to use Joseph, but Joseph's destiny was also tied to this dream and his interpretation of it.

God gives us revelations that He doesn't give unto others as we walk closely with Him. God gives us answers and solutions because He wants to use us. He wants us to be different and to make a difference. Just like Joseph's deliverance and destiny was tied to the dream and the interpretation of it, our blessings are tied to the solutions and answers that He gives to us, for others.

Pharaoh says to Joseph that he's the wisest (there is none so discreet and wise as thou art) and most capable person for the job.

People in high places of authority will recognize your ability if you allow God to use you. You will not have to promote yourself and elevate yourself, but even persons in great authority will gravitate towards you. Muhammad won't have to go to the mountain, but the mountain will come to Muhammad.

Thou shalt be over my house…

The King placed Joseph in charge of his entire house or Kingdom. Joseph went from being over his master's house as a slave, the prison as a prisoner, and now He was being placed over the entire kingdom of Egypt. You see, Joseph had a dream and he held on to his dream. I'm sure that

Joseph didn't have all the details of everything that would have occurred on his way to his destiny, if he had; he probably would have aborted his destiny. Somehow though, he believed God and he had God with him. This is what makes the difference, just knowing that God is with us.

The King of Kings will place us in charge. We will end up going from the servant's quarters to the king's palace as we continue to trust Him. We don't know how God is going to do it, but we do have a dream and we must hold on to our dream no matter what the enemy throws in front of us.

Joseph was given authority to rule over all of people of Pharaoh's kingdom. Joseph's word actually became law. Whatever Joseph would say, the king had confidence and trust in it. Like Joseph, God has given us authority to rule in the earth. Whatever we say, shall come to pass.

Listen to how Matthew puts it: (Matthew 16:13-20)
When Jesus came into the coasts of Caesarea Philippi, he asked his disciples, saying, Whom do men say that I the Son of man am? [14] And they said, Some say that thou art John the Baptist: some, Elias; and others, Jeremias, or one of the prophets. [15] He said unto them, But who say ye that I am? [16] And Simon Peter answered and said, Thou art the Christ, the Son of the living God. (Peter got a revelation of Jesus...Now what is Peter going to do about it...he's going to be used of God) [17] And Jesus answered and said unto him, Blessed art thou, Simon Barjona: for flesh and blood hath not revealed it unto thee, but my Father which is in heaven. [18] And I say also unto thee, That thou art Peter, and upon this rock I will build my church; and the gates of hell shall not prevail against it. [19] And I will give unto tee the keys of the kingdom of heaven: and whatsoever thou shalt bind on earth shall be bound in heave: and whatsoever thou shalt loose on earth shall be loosed in heaven.

Pharaoh reminded Joseph that he still was accountable to him (the King)...No matter how much authority the Lord gives us, we must remain accountable to Him. We must always remember that it's Him who's blessing us and not (us) ourselves...

The story tells us that Pharaoh placed his ring on Joseph's finger. This ring was a symbol of royal power and authority. The king's signature or signet was on this ring and Joseph had the power and authority to approve or disapprove every major political and economical decision in the land. When God elevates us, He allows us to use His name. We have the power and the authority to approve or disapprove things in the earth.

Because of Joseph's new status and authority, he was arrayed in fine clothing. His prosperity began to be evident and clear before everyone around. The clothes were symbols of his power and authority. Everything about Joseph's lifestyle began to change for the better.

Joseph, who had been a slave at one time; was now receiving tremendous honor because of the position or office he was placed in. People will ultimately honor us not because of the office and responsibility that has been placed on us.

Because Joseph did not forget his dream the Lord brought him out. Because Joseph did not forget the vision that God had given him, the Lord delivered him. Because Joseph was proactive and not reactive, he was destined for greatness.

Joseph knew what his gift was. Joseph knew how to take advantage of every opportunity that was before Him. Joseph knew how to position himself for greatness and Joseph knew how to not abort his promises. We can't allow the enemy to steal our dreams. We need to hold on to our dreams at all cost. Don't let anybody steal your dreams. Your dream is the solution to someone's problem. It is the answer that someone needs. Be proactive and take full responsibility for your own destiny, because you are destined for greatness. Understand your gift and know what your ability is and begin to work your stuff. Don't miss an opportunity. Take advantage of every opportunity that God gives you. Position yourself for greatness and don't abort the promise. Move from rags to riches. Move from poverty to blessings. Move from having no power to being powerful. Move from no authority to having great authority. Move from being weak to being strong. Move from having fear to having great faith.

Allow the Lord to make a difference in your life. You can't be afraid to be blessed and you can't allow people to keep you from your destiny. I am destined for greatness. You are destined for greatness. My whole lifestyle and your lifestyle is about to change as we allow God to use us to be "The solution to someone's problem."

CHAPTER NINE

STAY THE COURSE

*But recall the former days in which, after you were illuminated,
you endured a great struggle with sufferings: partly while you
were made a spectacle both by reproaches and tribulations, and
partly while you became companions of those who were so
treated; for you had compassion on me in my chains, and
joyfully accepted the plundering of your goods ,knowing that you
have a better and an enduring possession for yourselves in
heaven. Therefore do not cast away your confidence, which has
great reward.*
Hebrews 10:32-35

*But we are not of those who draw back to perdition, but of those
who believe to the saving of the soul.*
Hebrews 10:39

*Wherefore seeing we also are compassed about with so great a
cloud of witnesses, let us lay aside every weight, and the sin
which doth so easily beset us, and let us run with patience the
race that is set before us,*
Hebrews 12:1

If you have read The Book of Hebrews, you will
remember that chapter eleven talks about the heroes of
faith and their sufferings and hardships.
Can you imagine the great army of angels that surround
you? You may not be able to see them, but they are there.
Do you know that there is a sin that has been set before

you, to hinder you? It is good to know that we can overcome each and every one of them. How do you do this? By running with endurance and remaining in the race and by keeping your eyes on Jesus on whom your faith totally depends on from the beginning of the race, to the finish line. Jesus stayed in the race and was willing to die unto the end because He knew the joy He would experience afterwards. Now Jesus is seated in the place of the highest honor, beside God, on His throne in heaven.

The Book of Hebrews was written to address the doubts of those who were second guessing their conversion to Christianity. These people had come over from Judaism and some were leaning towards returning back to the world in which they had come from. You may be looking to go back or have a desire to go back to where you came from because it felt more comfortable to you. Life has a way of leading us in many directions. Often we must make difficult choices as to which path we are going to follow and what directions are lives are going to take. It's easy to get confused along the way and sometimes it is hard to know which path is the right one. Today, life offers us unlimited choices and possibilities, as a result temptation and confusion is a certainty. Right and wrong can easily become blurred. Things of true meaning and value can be overlooked and merely have the illusion of fulfillment. However, if we would remember the commitment that we have made and allow that commitment to guide us and to give us the strength to continue on we can all weather the storms that come our way." With all of the complexities, sudden changes to your routines, the curves that suddenly show up on your roads of life, and the pot holes that have been placed in your paths, every day, week, and hour you learn something new. Your life may appear to be a journey or a struggle. It may seem like the Holy Spirit is trying to press into your spirit. You may be considering giving up, or just falling off track. You may be at the point where you want to call on God and say, "Lord you have got to do something and come quickly because I am ready to give up". Sometimes the pains of going through may feel excruciating and you may even contemplate walking away from God. Stay encouraged and grab on with all that you've got.

In this journey you call life you will find yourself in a place where you can't figure out how, when, or what got you there. Every day pressures and demands can cause you to feel overwhelmed with life itself. You may have found yourself so over consumed with stuff that you lost sight of your primary purpose and goal. You may feel as though you have lost your bearings and have been thrown off course. Life can feel overwhelming especially when you have children and grandchildren who have a life of their own and they constantly pressure you into falling into their life. They generally don't understand that when you are caught up in the Spirit you can't come out unless God says so. They only want your undivided attention. Many times, your spouse doesn't even understand. This is why Paul says to put all of your time to God. It doesn't matter how anointed and holy you are. It doesn't matter how often you speak in tongues, dinner has to be cooked and dishes have to be washed. There are still things on top of what you already have to do that causes you to ponder on the question, "How did I get here?"

In today's society every one seems to be constantly busy. No one has time any more to sit down at the dinner table. No one sits down to fellowship like they did in the days of old. Preachers are throwing out quick sermons and not taking the time to teach a real Word any more. People are even praying quick and in a hurry. In today's society everybody wants what they want and they want it in a hurry. These types of things are distractions to your every day life and will throw you off track if you are not focused on the Lord; only He can keep you on course.

Just like the captain of a ship who uses the necessary instruments to determine his location and keep the ship on course; no matter what is going on in the ship the captain of the ship always remains focused on his job and is never distracted. In spite of all of the noises from the parties on the ship and all of the other noises that are derived from the sea, the captain remains focused. You see the captain never cares about what is going on around him. The captain always keeps his eye on the instruments. He has his destination in mind. No matter what happens in your life, even if you have death all around you, sickness in the atmosphere, or your family is acting up. Stay focused! Continue to run towards your destiny. Make up your mind, come hell or high water, come friend, for or not, know that you are going to get there. Fix your eyes not on man, but on God. Man will disappoint you and mess you up sometimes. It doesn't matter how much you love your fellow brothers or sisters, you have to stay focused on God. If you get too attached to man, many times your emotions alone will confuse you. Fix your eyes on Jesus and determine that He alone is your goal. Look to God, because God is the author and the finisher of your faith.

Interruptions will throw you off track sometimes. Think of those times when you are smooth sailing down the highways, or when you are on a cruise, and smoothly sailing along the ocean. Life is not always like that. Sometimes there are angry storms that rock your ship. Sometimes the storms of life make you have to grab a life jacket and put it on to weather the storms that rage in your life. Just stay focused. There are some folks in your life who enjoy the storm and want to take you with them. Stay focused! Don't get busy doing church work and not doing the work of the church. It's really easy to join the cliques that hang out there. Stay focused! Stop gossiping, back biting, and staying in other people's business, stay focused! Don't allow anything to destroy your focus and prevent you from reaching your place in destiny, Stay focused and stay the course.

CHAPTER TEN

WHAT GOD HAS FOR YOU, IS FOR YOU

Now his elder son was in the field: and as he came and drew nigh to the house, he heard musick and dancing. And he called one of the servants, and asked what these things meant. And he said unto him, Thy brother is come; and thy father hath killed the fatted calf, because he hath received him safe and sound. And he was angry, and would not go in: therefore came his father out, and intreated him. And he answering said to his father, Lo, these many years do I serve thee, neither transgressed I at any time thy commandment: and yet thou never gavest me a kid, that I might make merry with my friends: But as soon as this thy son was come, which hath devoured thy living with harlots, thou hast killed for him the fatted calf. And he said unto him, Son, thou art ever with me, and all that I have is thine. It was meet that we should make merry, and be glad: for this thy brother was dead and is alive again; and was lost, and is found.

Luke 15:25-32

This final chapter brings to mind that there seems to be pressure upon us at times to compete with others or to even be envious of others because of what they may have or possess, but as long as we remain in position for our blessing and favor, no one (but us) can abort our destinies. What God has done is to develop a system called inheritance to insure that each perpetual generation would be blessed. This is true in the secular society as well as in the Church.

The oldest male child was given the responsibility of securing prosperity for future generations by properly handling the natural resources and material blessings handed down from the father. Likewise, Jesus who is our Elder Brother has fulfilled the responsibility of handing down our inheritance from the father.

Proverbs 13:22 highlights this concept of inheritance. The scripture says a good man leaveth an inheritance to his children's children: and the wealth of the sinner is laid up for the just. Therefore, to not leave an inheritance is to be the opposite of good, and the opposite of good is evil or wicked. Jesus also tells us in the gospel that unprofitable servant is considered to be wicked. He was considered wicked because his bottom line was in the red. God literally holds us responsible for being profitable and creating an inheritance for our families.

It's never too late to get your inheritance back, but you must make some extra sacrifices.

In our story, we see a father being good but we also see a son being wicked, but restoration is always possible after revelation and repentance.

Notice the scripture: Luke 15:11-19 (This is how the story goes) And he said, A certain man had two sons: [12] and the younger of them said to his father, Father, give me the portion of goods that falleth to me. And he divided unto them his living. [13] And not many days after the younger son gathered all together, and took his journey into a far country.

This actually opened the door for this young man to be from around those persons who would hold him accountable. You need to be careful that you are not trying to escape accountability by getting a hold to your blessings prematurely and not have anyone to speak into your life and offer you suggestions for living.

The scripture says that this young man got involved with riotous or rebellious living which opened the door for all kinds of evil things to come into his life. This young man was living the so-called good life that was eating up his inheritance. He had fallen prey to many lies from the devil.

Instead of taking his money and reinvesting it, he blew it all as if there would never be a rainy day in his life. The scripture says that the famine didn't come until after he had spent all he had, and then came a mighty famine in the land. We should never live our lives thinking that we will never need some financial resources for emergencies.

This young man ended up in the wrong place at the wrong time. Isn't that how most of us get into trouble? The scripture says that this stranger helped the young man but the stranger looked out for himself first by placing this young man into the fields to feed swine. It's a shame but I've experienced many spiritually immature persons *leaving their place of inheritance* and blessing only to end up with strangers who didn't care as much for them as their spiritual father. Why do so many saints make that dumb mistake? Is there something inside of us such as a spirit of rebellion that causes us to leave a good and Godly thing for something less?

St. Luke Chapter 15 verses 16-18 bring these points out.

And he would fain have filled his belly with the husks that the swine did eat: and no man gave unto him. The devil had this young man down in the pig pen right along with the swine and finally the light comes on and he gets the revelation that he left his inheritance for a pipe dream, but listen to what he says in verses 17 and 18: And when he came to himself, he said, How many hired servants of my father's have bread enough and to spare, and I perish with hunger! I will arise and go to my father, and will say unto him, Father; I have sinned against heaven, and before thee. It's never too late to get your inheritance back, but you must make some extra sacrifices.

Notice: Luke 15:19-32. And am no more worthy to be called thy son: make me as one of thy hired servants. The younger son acknowledged his unworthiness to be called a son. What caused this acknowledgment of being unworthy? Through the difficulties of his life, he realized that he had made a serious mistake leaving home without the father's endorsement.

This endorsement concept is found in Matthew 3:13-17, as we see Jesus leaving Galilee for the purpose of participating in John's baptism as a candidate. This really pleased the father because Jesus forgot about his status and position as the Holy One of God and fulfills all righteousness by being obedient and having John, his lesser, to actually baptize Him. This is how the scripture puts it: [16] And Jesus, when he was baptized, went up straightway out of the water: and, lo, the heavens were opened unto him, and he saw the Spirit of God descending like a dove, and lighting upon him: [17] And lo a voice from heaven, saying, This is my beloved Son, in whom I am well pleased. If he (the prodigal son) desired to relocate, perhaps he should have requested that his father would have set him up in business in another town, rather than just getting his inheritance without a plan to increase it or maintain what he already had. Because of his poor decision making and stewardship, his status with the father had diminished, and he was willing to take on a job as a hired servant. If we are going to get ourselves together, we must acknowledge when our son-ship or daughter-ship has been jeopardized. We must acknowledge that we need son-ship and accountability in our lives to be successful. Most of all we need endorsement from someone other than ourselves. It's easy to see ourselves as the greatest thing since slice bread.

My greatest enemy could be in-me. God has ordained that we should be able to capitalize on our son-ship or daughter-ship and if we desire to move out into new territory. This endorsement concept is found in Matthew 3:13-17, this young man's father never lost his love and compassion for his son. As the boy was on his way back home, the father was anticipating his return so much that he met the young man half way and embraced him. A true father will somehow always be there for his children. Even though children get totally off track from time to time, a true father will never turn his back on his children. There is always room left in his heart for his children.

Here, the son confesses and acknowledges that he has totally messed up and says to the father that he is no more worthy to be called his son. It took a lot of courage on the part of the young man to acknowledge this. It will take a lot of courage on our part to acknowledge our mistakes, but it will be the very act that will get us back into position for our inheritance. Form the lessons drawn from Joseph's life we saw that one thing for certain was that Joseph positioned himself for his Godly inheritance by remaining faithful and in proper alignment with God. He made sure that he did not sin and do wickedness against God. In this story of the prodigal son, this young man comes to grips with the fact that he sinned against his father and heaven. When you sin against heaven you un-position yourself for blessings and prosperity.

In the text the father was so elated that his son finally came to his senses that he showered blessings all upon him. He placed the best robe upon him.

He put a ring on his hand and shoes on his feet. This young man was restored to his previous state of existence after throwing it all away. This scene reminds me of what happened to Joseph after he used his gift to solve the problems facing several nations. God is so elated when we finally come to our senses after periods of riotous and rebellious living. He places the robe upon us signifying unto us that we have been accepted back into the family and that we belong to His royalty. He gives us back our ring of authority, which is power over sin, the endowment to lay hands on the sick and see them recover, to speak with new tongues and cast out demons…Even the power to raise the dead. He tells us that whatever we bind on earth shall be bound in heaven and whatever we loose on earth shall be loosed in heaven.

A party was thrown for this young man upon his conversion and returned back home. As a matter of fact, the father took the choicest meat in the stock and threw a party on the behalf of his wayward son who had found himself and his purpose in life. Whenever a soul gets saved, the bible states that the angels in heaven our rejoicing and that a great cloud of witnesses (saints in glory) are cheering us on. We ought to be glad to see our brothers and sisters succeed. There ought not to be a hateful or jealous bone in our bodies.

This final chapter shows us that sometimes even our closet brothers and friends will sometimes miss it when God begins to forgive us and elevate us… Listen to verses 25-32 in our scripture.

[25] Now his elder son was in the field: and as he came and drew nigh to the house, he heard musick and dancing. [26] And he called one of the servants, and asked what these things meant. [27] And he said unto him, Thy brother is come; and thy father hath killed the fatted calf, because he hath received him safe and sound. [28] And he was angry, and would not go in: therefore came his father out, and intreated him. [29] And he answering said to his father, Lo, these many years do I serve thee, neither transgressed I at any time thy commandment: and yet thou never gavest me a kid, that I might make merry with my friends: [30] But as soon as this thy son was come, which hath devoured thy living with harlots, thou hast killed for him the fatted calf. [31] And he said unto him, Son, thou art ever with me, and all that I have is thine. [32] It was meet that we should make merry, and be glad: for this thy brother was dead and is alive again; and was lost, and is found.

There ought not to be a jealous or envious bone in our body if we have remained in proper order and alignment with the Father. Our inheritance is intact and no devils in hell can steal it from us. God tells us that we are forever with Him and all that He has belongs to us.

What a tremendous statement and what a tremendous revelation to know that we will spend eternity with God and everything that our Heavenly Father possesses, He has given us access to it, for we are heirs and joint heirs with Jesus Christ.

It's so exciting to know that God still looks beyond all my faults and meets my needs. It's so exciting to know that I can make immature choices and detrimental mistakes and still come out on the top in the end, if I repent. It's so exciting to know that I can blow all the money God gives me and fail to pay my tithes and offerings, but if I repent and turn it all around, then God can turn everything around for me. It's so exciting to know that if I'm humble enough and willing enough to lower myself, especially when I've done wrong, that God will be waiting for me with outstretched hands. He will dress me in royalty and give me back my authority over the enemy. I am destined for greatness. But the most important revelation about this story of the prodigal son is that the elder son who remained in proper position with the father didn't have to worry about a thing. His inheritance was intact and his relationship was intact, and most of all he didn't have to hate on his brother. You don't have to hate on anybody else. You don't have to be jealous of anybody else. You don't have to envious of anybody else. You don't have to compete with anybody else. You don't have to compare with anybody else. You don't have to complain about anybody else. What God has for you is for you and nobody can change that but you!

CONCLUSION

In conclusion, I would like to say that writing this book has been a tremendous experience. Many of the principles that have been shared in this book have come from a faith walk and practical experience of my own Christian lifestyle. I have no doubt that God has positioned me for greatness, but as I have shared with you in these pages; you should be totally aware that God has also destined you for greatness. Over the last 15 years of my life, I have had the privilege of being able to hear from God and move as He speaks. He has shown me the importance of being a problem solver and attempting to be a blessing in other's lives. As we make up our minds to serve God and his people to our greatest capacity, He will continue to endow us with the gifts and talents we need to minister to others. After all, life is most fulfilling when we are able to bring joy into other people's lives. We must all start out with the minimal resources that we have and not use our smallness as an excuse for not launching out into our destiny. Therefore I have tried to convey unto you that we must not despise small beginnings. Also, I have borrowed the thoughts of my wife, as she teaches us to stay the course and continue to persevere regardless of the obstacles that may be in front of us. These and many other principles have been the substance of this book. Study the scriptures and principles outlined in this book and you can be guaranteed that you are destined for greatness.

Still

DESTINED FOR
GREATNESS

ABOUT THE AUTHOR

Bishop Aubrey G. Mullen, Jr. is indeed a man of great integrity. After being faced with many challenges in his life, he still presses forward to do the work of the Lord! His primary focus of ministry is to reach the un-reached and to disciple the un-discipled through global missions and worldwide evangelism. He is committed to work until the Lord's return. His utmost desire is to fulfill the Great Commission.

He is a native of Chesapeake, Virginia and now resides in Jacksonville, NC. He and his wife Vanessa have been blessed with four beautiful children, Canita, Christopher (deceased), Krystal and Gerard; they also have four beautiful granddaughters, N'Jaria Abria-Joi, Abria Louisa, Kristeon Vanessa and Nyjah, as well as two handsome grandsons, Christopher Joseph and Aydan. He is a graduate of Christian Leadership Seminary in Elma, New York with a Master of Theology Degree and a Doctorate of Divinity degree. He is the pastor of Abundant Life International Baptist Cathedral in Jacksonville, NC. On June 16, 2001, he was installed as the Southeast District Overseer of the Full Gospel Baptist Church Fellowship International (FGBCFI) of North Carolina. In March of 2005, he was elevated to the office of Bishop-Elect for the State of North Carolina. In July of 2005, he was consecrated to the office of Bishop.

He provides continuous financial, agricultural, and medical support to churches he has planted abroad. He also conducts an annual mission's trip to minister to, as well as to witness first hand, the needs of God's people.

CELEBRATING LEGACY

*Eccentric...Unusual...AvantGarde... **describes** him...*

Radical...Revolutionary... Renaissance... ***defines*** the Ministry, the Mission, and the Man - Bishop Aubrey G. Mullen, Jr., the set man of Abundant Life International Baptist Cathedral, Jacksonville NC. Bishop Mullen functions and flourishes in ministry alongside his wife, Co Pastor Vanessa H. Mullen.

As an author, he penned his first book, "Destined for Greatness" to push the body of Christ into discovering and walking into their destiny. As the anointed of God, he is called upon often to minister across the country to the masses.

FAMILY: Together, they are blessed with their children, Canita, Christopher (deceased), Krystal, and Gerard; and their grandchildren, N'Jaria Abria-Joi, Abria Louisa, Kristeon Vanessa, Nyjah, Christopher Joseph and Aydan.

FIVE-FOLD: Graced and Gifted, Called and Chosen, Bishop Mullen flows in the five-fold ministry as ***APOSTLE***...in 1994, with only 55 members, he established Abundant Life International Baptist Cathedral which has impacted the lives for over 1000. Through his ministry, Abundant Life of Havelock and Goldsboro were birthed and churches were planted in Zimbabwe, Mozambique and South Africa...as ***PROPHET***, he speaks the heart of God with clarity as he decrees and declares what thus saith Lord...as ***PASTOR***, he not only shepherds thousands but he is a

Pastor's Pastor – imparting into many sons and daughters...as *EVANGELIST*, he has traveled the globe to implore lost souls to "repent for the Kingdom of God is at hand"...as *TEACHER*, Bishop Mullen instructs the weekly "Hour of Power" and new members training as he develop disciples for the work of the ministry. He also serves as president, of Abundant Life Christian College.

FELLOWSHIP: On June 16, 2006, he was installed as the Southeast District Overseer of the Full Gospel Baptist Church Fellowship International of North Carolina. In July 2005, he was consecrated to the office of Bishop in the Lord's church.

FOCUS: His primary focus of ministry is to reach the un-reached and to disciple the undiscipled through global missions and worldwide evangelism. He is committed to work until the Lord's return. His utmost desire is to fulfill the Great Commission.

www.alibc.com